CW01643395

GALE
CENGAGE Learning

Novels for Students, Volume 34

Project Editor: Sara Constantakis Rights Acquisition and Management: Beth Beaufore, Sara Crane, Leitha Etheridge-Sims, Barb McNeil Composition: Evi Abou-El-Seoud Manufacturing: Drew Kalasky

Imaging: John Watkins

Product Design: Pamela A. E. Galbreath, Jennifer Wahi Content Conversion: Katrina Coach Product Manager: Meggin Condino © 2010 Gale, Cengage Learning ALL RIGHTS RESERVED. No part of this work covered by the copyright herein may be reproduced, transmitted, stored, or used in any form or by any means graphic, electronic, or mechanical, including but not limited to photocopying, recording, scanning, digitizing, taping, Web distribution, information networks, or information storage and retrieval systems, except as permitted under Section 107 or 108 of the 1976 United States Copyright Act, without the prior written permission of the publisher.

Since this page cannot legibly accommodate all copyright notices, the acknowledgments constitute an extension of the copyright notice.

For product information and technology assistance, contact us at **Gale Customer Support, 1-800-877-4253.**
For permission to use material from this text or product, submit all requests online at www.cengage.com/permissions.
Further permissions questions can be emailed to **permissionrequest@cengage.com** While every effort has been made to ensure the reliability of the information presented in this publication, Gale, a part of Cengage Learning, does not guarantee the accuracy of the data contained herein. Gale accepts no payment for listing; and inclusion in the publication of any organization, agency, institution, publication, service, or individual does not imply endorsement of the editors or publisher. Errors brought to the attention of the publisher and verified to the satisfaction of the publisher will be corrected in future editions.

Gale
27500 Drake Rd.
Farmington Hills, MI, 48331-3535

ISBN-13: 978-1-4144-4172-6
ISBN-10: 1-4144-4172-X
ISSN 1094-3552

This title is also available as an e-book.
ISBN-13: 978-1-4144-4950-0

ISBN-10: 1-4144-4950-X
Contact your Gale, a part of Cengage Learning sales representative for ordering information.

Printed in the United States of America
1 2 3 4 5 6 7 14 13 12 11 10

A Handful of Dust

Evelyn Waugh 1934

Introduction

Although it is not Evelyn Waugh's most famous work, many critics consider *A Handful of Dust*, published in 1934, to be his finest novel. Written in a scathing if understated style, *A Handful of Dust* skewers the English high society of the years between the world wars. Waugh, who himself was a product of elite schools and the London social scene, had poked fun at modern society in earlier novels as well. But in *A Handful of Dust* Waugh employs satire and irony as a way of dealing with issues both more personal and more meaningful than mere social criticism. In his telling of the break-up of the marriage of Tony and Brenda Last, Waugh deals with his feelings of shame and humiliation after the collapse of his first marriage a few years before. At the same time, Waugh uses the story of Tony Last to ask broader questions about the role of tradition in English society as well as the value of the more modern and materialistic culture of the 1920s and 1930s. Waugh had converted to Catholicism shortly before he began the novel and, although there is little explicit mention of religion in the book, it is a highly moral story, exhibiting what Waugh believed to be the utter emptiness of secular, modern life.

Author Biography

Evelyn Arthur St. John Waugh was born in 1903, in London, England. His father was Arthur Waugh, a publisher and biographer, and his brother was Alec Waugh, also a novelist. Waugh attended the elite secondary school, Lancing College, where he edited the school's literary magazine, before enrolling in Hertford College at Oxford University. Not an outstanding student, Waugh tended to focus on art and his social life rather than on his studies. While still at the university, Waugh published short stories in student periodicals. After graduation, Waugh co-produced the 1924 film *The Scarlet Woman, An Ecclesiastical Melodrama*. In the years that followed Waugh struggled to settle into a career, studying art and teaching at a number of secondary schools. In his early twenties, Waugh was heavily depressed, drank far too much alcohol, and considered (and perhaps even attempted) suicide. All the while he continued an active social life in London's fashionable circles of young people, and he would mine both this world as well as that of elite schools for much of the material in his early novels.

In 1927, Waugh's life took a new turn as he fell in love with the aristocratic Evelyn Gardner, the daughter of Lord Burghclere. The family of Ms. Gardner, who became known by many friends as "she-Evelyn," was strongly opposed to Waugh's romantic interests as the two Evelyns became increasingly intimate. Waugh received a contract to write a biography of the poet and painter Dante Gabriel Rossetti that same year. Although Waugh wrote the book hurriedly, it received largely positive reviews. While finishing the Rossetti biography, Waugh began writing the manuscript for his first novel, *Decline and Fall*. The following year the Evelyns were secretly married, though the relationship would soon sour.

In 1928, *Decline and Fall*m a wickedly sharp satire of the life of the upper class, appeared to rave reviews, and Waugh's career as a novelist was promisingly launched. He also wrote numerous articles for newspapers and magazines and managed a growing public reputation. His personal life suffered, however, as he learned of his wife's infidelity. Much like the marriage of Tony and Brenda Last in *A Handful of Dust*, the Waughs' marriage crumbled when Evelyn secluded himself (in his case, to finish a novel) and his wife enjoyed the London party scene. There she fell in love with another man and told Evelyn so in a letter. Their marriage ended soon after.

In part as a reaction to his rejection by his wife, and in part fulfilling a long-held dissatisfaction with modern English life, Waugh converted to Catholicism and was received officially into the Church in 1930. From this point on, his novels would be deeply affected by his religious faith. They would also reflect his worldwide travel, often done as a journalist, which resulted in popular works of travel writing. His novels continued to be comic and satirical, often at the expense of the English elite. *A Handful of Dust*, which appeared in 1934, was no exception and also contained a scathing though disguised portrait of his marriage. When the Catholic Church annulled Waugh's first marriage in 1936, he quickly married again, this time to Laura Herbert, also a member of the English gentry. Herbert's family had converted to Catholicism and the match was ideal for the ambitious and religious Waugh. With the earnings from his novels, Waugh purchased a country estate, where he and Laura raised six children.

As the clouds of war gathered over Europe in the late 1930s, Waugh took the unpopular stand of supporting the Italian invasion of Ethiopia as well as the fascist side in the Spanish Civil War. No fascist himself, Waugh saw it as preferable to Marxism and the lesser of two evils. When England went to war against fascism in 1939, Waugh joined the Royal Marines. His experiences in battle became the basis for his highly regarded wartime novels, including *Put Out More Flags*m published in 1942, and *Brideshead Revisited*, published in 1945. It was this latter novel that would solidify Waugh's reputation in the United States, and it remains his most popular work.

After the war, Waugh settled into the life of a famous and respected novelist. He toured the United States, giving lectures. Yet the postwar American world order and the Labour government in England sickened the traditional Waugh, and he felt increasingly estranged from modern society. These feelings were reflected in his novels of the 1950s and 1960s. Seen by many as increasingly cranky and out of step, Waugh became disheartened with the democratization of England and even of the Catholic Church itself. Waugh died on April 10, 1966, after attending a Latin mass in Somerset. As biographer Calvin Lane wrote, "To the end, he remained a complex, often difficult, idiosyncratic person who could not and would not accommodate himself to the temper of contemporary British life."

Plot Summary

Chapter 1: Du Côté de Chez Beaver

A Handful of Dust opens with Mrs. Beaver and her son John discussing a house fire. At first it appears they are concerned with the victims of the fire. It quickly becomes clear, however, that Mrs. Beaver's interest in the fire is financial: she wants to sell the victims' home furnishings. John, who lives with his mother, is waiting for a phone call, not from anyone in particular but rather for an invitation to lunch. Since the beginning of the "slump," what Americans call the Great Depression, he has been idle as "no one had been able to find anything for him to do." John and Mrs. Beaver discuss various members of high society and their contacts with them. Clearly, Beaver (as Waugh calls him), is peripheral to this world but labors for acceptance. He mentions that he has been invited to visit Tony Last and his wife for the weekend at their country estate, Hetton, and Mrs. Beaver advises that he reply with a telegram because it will give them no chance to back out of the invitation. The two discuss the Lasts in a somewhat critical way, though Beaver clearly intends to take advantage of their hospitality.

After Beaver receives a phone call from a lady who wants to know the name of someone Beaver knows so she can invite this other man to lunch, the scene shifts to Beaver's club, Brat's, a place at which he is not very popular. He runs into the handsome and wealthy Jock Grant-Menzies, who is a member of Parliament. They chat about the Lasts, and Jock assures Beaver that he will like Brenda Last. "I often think Tony Last's one of the happiest men I know," he continues. "He's got just enough money, loves the place, one son he's crazy about, devoted wife, not a worry in the world." Beaver checks his messages and discovers he has received a last-minute invitation to lunch. He hurriedly leaves Brat's.

Chapter 2: English Gothic-I

The chapter begins with a guidebook description of the Lasts' house, Hetton Abbey. Hetton was renovated in the 1860s in a faux-medieval style and is therefore "devoid of interest." Tony, however, loves the house and is sure it will be considered stylish again someday. It matches his boyish enthusiasm for the England of King Arthur. In fact, he names the bedrooms after characters in the Arthurian legends—Guinevere, Lancelot, and so on.

Media Adaptations

- *A Handful of Dust,* adapted as a film by Charles Sturridge and starring James Wilby, Kristin Scott Thomas, and Anjelica Huston, was released by New Line Cinema in 1988. It was nominated for an Oscar that year.
- *A Handful of Dust* was also adapted for the London stage by Mike Alfreds in 1982. The play was revived to mostly positive reviews in 2005.

Tony and Brenda seem very happy together, eating breakfast as she reads him the papers. Although Brenda seems less enthusiastic about staying in the country, their life together seems almost perfect. Outside, their son, John Andrew, rides his horse under the tutelage of Ben Hacket, who looks after the horses at Hetton. John falls from the horse but is not hurt and after more effort clears a jump. John's nanny, who is also present, is insulted by John, and she sends him to the nursery. Brenda speaks to John about this but he is disrespectful, telling her he likes Ben more than anyone else. Brenda reminds John he is a gentleman, though she later admits her scolding is a failure.

Later, Tony and Brenda receive Beaver's telegram and struggle to remember much about him. They decide to put him in the Sir Galahad bedroom because it is uncomfortable. When Beaver arrives, Tony slips off on business and Brenda entertains him. On Sunday, Tony again slips away from Beaver and enjoys his ritual visit to church. While he has little or no religious feeling, Tony enjoys listening to the reverend's sermons, although they were written and first delivered when he was overseas and bear no relation to English life. Tony also enjoys chatting after church, walking home, pausing in the hothouses for a flower for his buttonhole, and then having dinner before retiring for sherry in his library. It is a routine that pleases Tony very much.

On his return from church, Tony finds Beaver telling Brenda's fortune. Tony takes Beaver on a two-hour tour of the house, which Beaver appears to enjoy greatly. Back with his mother, Beaver admits he would like to see more of Brenda. He tells his mother that Brenda is thinking of finding a flat in

London. Mrs. Beaver is sure she could find Brenda something to her liking.

Brenda impulsively visits her sister Marjorie in London. Brenda tells of Beaver's visit. When Marjorie asks if she "fancies" Beaver, Brenda says, "Heavens, no." Later she admits she is attracted to him. They see Mrs. Beaver in a restaurant and briefly discuss a flat for Brenda. Beaver accompanies Brenda to the train station but the potentially romantic moment falls flat. The next day he telegrams her at Hetton, asking her to a party. She replies that she is "delighted." Tony notices her high spirits.

Beaver arrives at Marjorie's home to pick up Brenda for Lady Cockpurse's party. They bicker about who will pay for dinner as Beaver wonders if he should try to kiss Brenda. Both seem to have accepted the fact that they are beginning an affair. They chat excitedly at a restaurant and kiss in the taxi. As she had earlier with Tony, Brenda rubs Beaver's cheek "in the way she had." They enjoy the party. Beaver takes Brenda back to Marjorie's home. She calls him a little later but again he seems incapable of romantic talk.

The next morning Brenda tells Marjorie that the evening before was quite innocent and that she fears Beaver found her boring. She admits she finds him "as cold as a fish." When Beaver does not call her she believes their affair is over. But they run into each other at a restaurant at lunchtime and decide to see a movie. Afterward, Brenda telegrams Tony, saying she is staying with Marjorie for a few more days.

Brenda returns to Hetton and tells Tony she has been "behaving badly" and "carrying on madly with young men" while spending "heaps of money." She also tells him she has found a flat she wants in London. Tony is against it, feeling they cannot afford it and do not need it. Three days later she is back in London, where the social scene was abuzz with news of her affair with Beaver. Brenda takes the flat against her sister's advice and, once there, calls Tony. He is disappointed but sends her flowers. Beaver goes to Ireland for Christmas and Brenda is bored at Hetton. When Tony asks her if her New Year's resolution is to spend more time at home she tells him that, quite the opposite, she intends to spend more time away, perhaps enrolling in a course in economics.

Chapter 3: Hard Cheese on Tony

Jock Grant-Menzies finds Tony eating and drinking alone at Brat's. Together they get drunk while Tony unhappily talks mostly of Brenda. Brenda has Beaver call Tony, pretending to be a servant, saying she has gone to bed early. Tony calls back and tells Brenda he is coming to her flat. Brenda calls Brat's and tells Jock to keep Tony away. Jock tries to convince Tony to go to Brenda's but they end up at a seedy nightclub called 64. There Tony and Jock meet two young women named Milly and Babs who may or may not be prostitutes. Tony and Jock continue to argue about going to Brenda's, ending up at Jock's. The next day, Tony calls Brenda and apologizes for his drunken calls. She tells Beaver that all this is fortunate because Tony will now leave her alone. Tony returns to Hetton, feeling guilty. Alone, he sleeps in Brenda's room.

Brenda returns from London with Polly Cockpurse, her friend Veronica, and Mrs. Beaver. They essentially ignore Tony, insulting Hetton and talking of renovating it. Brenda talks about her flat as if she has moved there permanently. On Saturday night Brenda tells Tony she has drunk too much and cannot speak with him. The next morning she sleeps in and he goes to church alone. The next day, the women try to plan an affair for Tony. Brenda sends a woman called Jenny Abdul Akbar to Hetton, hoping she and Tony will become involved. Tony, who has no idea of the plan, greets her as a guest of Brenda, whom he expects to follow shortly. He does not like Jenny, who inexplicably calls him "Teddy." She is uncouth and pretentious and Tony is relieved when John enters. The boy speaks frankly with Jenny and later tells his nanny he thinks she is the most beautiful woman he has ever seen. Brenda arrives and encourages Jenny despite her poor start. The next morning, John finds Jenny in Galahad; he is clearly smitten with her. Jenny goes to church with Tony and he almost warms to her. Still, the scheme for romance is a complete failure. Tony is worried that their marriage is not going well but Brenda tells him not to brood. Clearly lonely, he begs Jock to extend a weekend visit. Jock cheers up Tony, which makes Brenda feel better about her treatment of him.

Jock's lover, an American named Mrs. Rattery, arrives at Hetton as the house is in preparation for an annual hunt. John begs to be as involved with the hunt as possible though the adults only want him there at the beginning. A young local woman, Miss Ripon, is also at the hunt, though she struggles with her horse. The hunt is called off and John is sent home. As they ride back to Hetton, Miss Ripon, Ben, and John are involved in an accident and John is struck by a horse's hoof. He is killed instantly. Tony sends Jock to tell Brenda and tries to make funeral arrangements. Mrs. Rattery waits behind to comfort Tony, who in turn worries about Brenda.

Tony struggles with the fact that he knows of John's death so long before Brenda. He wants to tell the extended family but also wants to wait until he knows Brenda has heard. Mrs. Rattery tries to help him forget his trouble by having Tony play silly children's games. Tony is embarrassed and the servants are scandalized. Jock arrives at Brenda's and meets Jenny Abdul Akbar. She inexplicably blames herself for John's death, claiming that wherever she goes bad things happen. Jenny then begins to feel sorry for herself. Jock and Jenny find Brenda at a party where a number of women are having their fortunes told. Alone, Jock tells Brenda that John is dead. Brenda thinks he means John Beaver and when Jock clears up the misunderstanding, Brenda says, "Oh thank God." She weeps but it is unclear that it is not from relief. Returning to Hetton, Brenda keeps to herself. She tells Tony that their life at Hetton is "over," though he does not see why. Tony talks to Jock about Brenda's puzzling behavior: she has gone off to Veronica's. There she tells Beaver that she now realizes she loves him though he seems unmoved. The following Monday, Tony receives a letter from Brenda announcing that she is not coming back to Hetton, that she loves John Beaver, and that she wants a divorce. Tony does not fully understand the letter for several days.

Chapter 4: English Gothic-II

Tony is bombarded by friends and relatives who try to make peace between the married couple. A phone call with Brenda makes Tony realize the relationship is over. In order to give Brenda a divorce, Tony decides that he will allow her to portray herself as the wronged party. His lawyer, who does not share Tony's faith in Brenda, advises him to get all agreements in writing. It is decided that Tony will pretend to have an affair and that private detectives will collect evidence against him. At first he struggles to come up with a woman to help him. Jock suggests they return to 64 and there they meet up again with Milly and Babs. The women have taken part in such arrangements before and Milly agrees to accompany Tony to Brighton, a beachside resort, if her young daughter can also come along. Tony is aghast at the idea and says no.

Tony, Milly, and the private detectives meet later at a train station. Tony is angered to see Milly's daughter, Winnie, with her, but he is unable to prevent her from coming. At the hotel, the detectives look on disapprovingly on this new twist and they tell Tony of their feelings when he joins them for a drink in the hotel bar. For his part, Tony feels that his world has suddenly become "bereft of order," so farcical are the events in his life now. Dan, a friend of Milly, arrives with his girlfriend Baby, and Tony joins them for a party.

Early the next morning, Winnie wakes Tony and demands they go to the beach. Back at the hotel, Tony eats breakfast in the dining room, only to be told by one of the detectives that they need more evidence. So Tony goes back upstairs and pretends to eat breakfast in bed with Milly. Returning from the trip, Tony meets with Reggie St. Cloud, Brenda's brother. A stout man who seems much older than he truly is, Reggie is an archaeologist and a member of the House of Lords. Reggie, who had been in Tunisia until he heard about the affair, accuses Tony of being vindictive and of pushing Brenda and Beaver together. Reggie lectures Tony about drinking too much and seeing other women. For Tony, this talk seems a continuation of his surreal life of late. Finally, Reggie demands Tony quadruple his proposed annual payment to Brenda. Tony protests that this would mean giving up Hetton and that Brenda would never want him to do that. Tony defends Brenda to Reggie but when he calls her she confirms that this is her wish. The conversation is a turning point for Tony. "A whole Gothic world had come to grief.... "His vision of his life at Hetton now shattered, Tony asserts that there will be no divorce and that he is going away.

Chapter 5: In Search of a City

The scene shifts to the deck of a ship bound for Trinidad. Tony meets a man who asks him why he is traveling. When Tony tells him he is "looking for a city," the man is a bit put off. Soon, however, Tony gains a reputation with the other passengers as an explorer. He has left England because he believes that is what a person in his circumstances should do. Tony had met Dr. Messinger, a young bearded man who tells him he is on his way to Brazil to search for a fabled city in the heart of the South American continent. Tony, who had planned to go on a simple cruise, had torn up his pamphlets and joined Dr. Messinger on his quest. In Tony's mind the city is "Gothic in character, all vanes and pinnacles, … a transfigured Hetton…. "

Also on the ship is a young woman named Thérèe de Vitré, returning to Trinidad after years of studying in Paris in order to marry. She asks Tony about his exploring and they become friends, playing shuffleboard and other games. Nearing Barbados their relationship becomes romantic. They kiss and she asks him to visit her in Trinidad. This changes suddenly when he tells her he is married. Thérèe, a strict Catholic, is horrified and does not introduce him to her father when he greets her in Trinidad. In town, Tony sees her. She waves but does not stop to speak to him. Another passenger assures him this is typical of the local elites.

For some time during the chapter, the scene shifts back and forth between Tony's journey and events back in London. Tony and Dr. Messinger chug upstream toward "the City." Tony is tortured by the many biting insects and small animals of the jungle. Meanwhile Brenda, out dancing with Jock, says she is still fond of Tony despite his behavior. Tony camps in an Indian village, waiting for the men to return. Jock worries about the dumping of low-price pork pies on the English market. Tony hunts with the Indians and thinks of his old history teacher. Beaver admits to his mother that he does not know where his relationship with Brenda is going. Tony and Dr. Messinger walk for two weeks, speaking rarely because of their exhaustion. Mrs. Beaver suggests John should have a holiday.

Tony and Dr. Messinger's supplies run low and their Indian guides refuse to hunt because of fears of evil spirits. Dr. Messinger repeatedly asks their interpreter, Rosa, when their canoes will be ready. He cannot get a straight answer from her. Finally, she declares that the men will go no farther, though the canoes are now ready. Dr. Messinger tries to entice them with mechanical toy mice. When he demonstrates them, the Indians run away into the bush. Brenda and Beaver bicker about his intention to travel to America with his mother. The Indians desert Tony and Dr. Messinger. "The situation is grave," says Tony's companion.

Tony and Dr. Messinger travel on together, down the treacherous river. Tony develops a fever, which comes and goes, making him delirious. One afternoon he has a vision of Brenda. Dr. Messinger nurses him. He leaves in his canoe to look for a sign of a village nearby. Approaching rapids, he tries to get to the bank, but tips over, falls over a waterfall, and dies of his injuries. Brenda sees the family lawyer in the hopes of receiving more money. Instead she learns that Tony has made a new will, leaving Hetton to his cousins. Alone in the jungle and feeling unwell, Tony begins to cry. His fever returns. Brenda realizes that her affair with Beaver is over. She breaks down. Tony dreams surreal dreams, in which Rosa, Milly, Lady Cockpurse, and others discuss the widening of a road. Brenda declares her love for Beaver. Voices come and go. Finally, Tony sees a vision of "the City." It is like a gothic castle with ramparts and battlements. Tony stumbles through the jungle toward his hallucination of a shining version of the Hetton of his imagination.

Chapter 6: Du Côté de Chez Todd

Tony is rescued by a Mr. Todd, a man of European descent who has lived in the Amazon for almost sixty years. Mr. Todd humors the hallucinating Tony and gives him medicine that makes him sleep. After several days he feels much better. Tony asks Mr. Todd about his background. Todd claims to be the father of most of the people in the area. He is the most powerful man in the region but is ashamed that he cannot read. He asks Tony to read to him. Tony learns that Mr. Todd has a great fondness for the novelist Charles Dickens and has many of his books. At first Tony enjoys reading Dickens's novels to Mr. Todd, but he begins to find his host somewhat threatening. When he asks about a canoe to return downriver, Mr. Todd is evasive. Tony finds a note from an earlier visitor who seems to have shared his predicament. As Tony presses for a boat, Mr. Todd begins to hold his shotgun on his lap when they are reading. After they are visited by a prospector, Tony is cheered because he feels he may be rescued soon. Mr. Todd gives Tony a local drink that causes him to sleep for two days. When he wakes he discovers a rescue party has come and gone. Mr. Todd has let on that Tony had died. He is stuck with Mr. Todd forever.

Chapter 7: English Gothic-III

Tony's cousin, Richard Last, now runs Hetton. The staff has been reduced and life there is simpler. Over an informal breakfast with his family, he reads a letter from "Cousin Brenda." She writes to say that she cannot attend the dedication of a memorial to Tony. She is stuck in London where her new husband, Jock Grant Menzies, has business before Parliament. Later that morning, Reverend Tendril unveils a memorial to "Anthony Last of Hetton, Explorer." The novel closes with one of the Last children, twenty-two-year-old Teddy, dreaming that someday he can restore Hetton to its former glory under his cousin Tony.

Characters

Jenny Abdul Akbar

Jenny is a shallow and emotional woman in Brenda's circle of friends. Brenda sends her to Hetton to try to have an affair with Tony, but she fails. Jenny irrationally and selfishly thinks John's death is her fault because of her very presence. Despite her declarations of deep fondness for Brenda, she drifts away from her after Tony's departure leaves Brenda with little money.

Allan

Allan is Marjorie's husband, Brenda's brother-in-law. He takes a dim view of Brenda's affair with Beaver. Like Marjorie, he is "hard up and smart."

Babs

Babs is one of two young women Tony and Jock meet when they spend an evening drinking at the nightclub 64. She is surprised when the men do not go home with them.

Baby

Baby is the girlfriend of Milly's friend Dan. She meets Tony at the hotel in Brighton. She is distressed because she sees people she believes to be Jewish at the hotel.

John Beaver

Usually referred to as "Beaver" in the novel, John Beaver is a somewhat handsome but rather dull young man on the outskirts of British high society. With little money, he is compelled to live with his ambitious mother. Beaver drifts in and out of his relationship with Brenda Last with seemingly little emotion. His speech is clipped and repetitive. He seems incapable of emotion, even when he writes his lover, Brenda, a note of thanks for a lovely ring she has given him for Christmas. When it is clear that Brenda will not make him rich, Beaver goes with his mother to America, though it is fairly clear that even this was not originally his idea.

Mrs. Beaver

Mrs. Beaver is an ambitious businesswoman who uses her social contacts to further her interior design business. She appears to be without any interest besides furthering her own career and the amorous adventures of her son. It is she who pushes Beaver into the affair with Brenda Last and suggests the trip to America as a way of bringing it to an end.

Lady Polly Cockpurse

Despite her aristocratic title, Polly Cockpurse

is shallow and boorish. She convinces Brenda that Tony needs to have an affair and disastrously chooses Jenny Abdul Akbar for the job.

Dan

Dan is a friend of Milly whom she and Tony chance upon at the hotel in Brighton.

Jock Grant-Menzies

Jock is Tony's best friend and a member of Parliament. Jock is a highly eligible bachelor and had been considered a likely match for Brenda before she married Tony. Tony turns to Jock when he is confused over Brenda's decision to get a flat in London. It is also Jock who travels from Hetton to London to tell Brenda of John Andrew's death.

Ben Hacket

Ben is a worldly man who looks after the stables at Hetton. He is John Andrew Last's hero and described by Waugh as "a man of varied experience in other parts of the country."

James and Blenkinsop

Detectives hired to record Tony's pretended infidelity. They travel to Brighton where they befriend Tony despite company rules.

Brenda Last

Brenda is Tony Last's wife, a pale beauty who had been considered one of the most eligible young women on the London social scene before her marriage. She is not happy living at Hetton, finding life there secluded and boring, though at the beginning of the novel she appears to have a perfectly happy marriage. The events of the story show her to be self-centered and self-deluding as she somehow comes to see herself as the victim of Tony's poor behavior.

John Andrew Last

The only child of Brenda and Tony Last, John is a precocious and painfully honest young boy. He speaks his mind openly to guests at Hetton, often embarrassing his parents. He is interested only in horses and idolizes Ben Hacket, who looks after the Lasts' stable. John begs his parents to take part in the annual hunt. They allow him to watch and stay out of the action, but he is killed in an accident nevertheless.

Richard Last

Richard is Tony's poorer cousin who inherits Hetton after Tony alters his will. At the end of the novel, Richard is raising silver foxes at Hetton and living there with his less aristocratic family.

Teddy Last

Teddy is Richard Last's twenty-two-year-old son who lives with his parents at Hetton at novel's end. Like Tony before him, he dreams of restoring Hetton to its previous glory, though in his mind it is Tony who is the model to be imitated.

Tony Last

Tony is the somewhat pathetic hero of the novel. He is the lord of a manor house, Hetton, and wants nothing except to live there comfortably. He has never really grown up and fantasizes about the romantic past of his family and his house. He is devoted to his wife, Brenda, but is clueless about her unhappiness at Hetton. Tony is the character readers sympathize with, but his romantic nature and his blindness to the reality around him make him less than heroic.

Marjorie

Marjorie is Brenda's younger sister. She is against Brenda's affair with Beaver. She lives in a small flat in Partman Square with her husband, Allan.

Dr. Messinger

Dr. Messinger is a young, bearded explorer who leads Tony on his adventure in search of "the City." He believes he understands the Indians' minds and this overconfidence leads to his death.

Milly

Milly is one of the young women Tony and Jock meet at the club 64. When Tony struggles to think of someone to have his supposed infidelity with, he settles on Milly. They travel to Brighton but Milly insists on bringing her young daughter along for the trip.

Mrs. Rattery

The American Mrs. Rattery is Jock Grant Menzies's lover. She is an able card player and an occasional morphine user. She makes a splash by arriving at Hetton in a plane, but she fails to console Tony after John Andrew's accident.

Miss Ripon

Miss Ripon, a pretty local girl, rides a nervous horse her father hopes to sell at the hunt. She is involved in John's accident.

Rosa

Rosa is the Indian guide and interpreter hired by Tony and Dr. Messinger. She continuously demands cigarettes and often confuses and confounds the Englishmen with her statements.

Lady St. Cloud

Brenda's mother, who, although she had not initially been keen on Brenda's choice of Tony for a husband, feels her daughter's extramarital affair is foolish.

Reggie St. Cloud

Reggie St. Cloud is Brenda's heavy-set brother who returns from Tunisia to convince Tony to accept her demand that Tony give up Hetton. Reggie only succeeds in angering Tony and scuttling the divorce settlement.

Reverend Tendril

Reverend Tendril is the vicar at Tony's church. He seemed to believe he was preaching to Britons in India. The parishioners seem not to notice his references to exile from home and to Queen Victoria, who had died thirty years before.

Mr. Todd

Mr. Todd lives with the Pie-Wie Indians and saves Tony's life after the death of Dr. Messinger. He has lived in the jungle about sixty years and, unlike Dr. Messinger, is familiar with the environment and people. He claims to be the father of most of the Indians in the vicinity. Mr. Todd nurses Tony back to health but then imprisons him, demanding Tony read him the novels of Charles

Dickens.

Veronica

Veronica is a friend of Lady Cockpurse who visits Hetton and criticizes its furnishings.

Thérèe de Vitré

Tony meets this slight young woman aboard ship. She is returning to Trinidad from two years studying in Paris and is intending to find a husband. They strike up a shipboard romance but she abruptly drops Tony when she discovers he is married.

Winnie

Winnie is Milly's eight-year-old daughter who tags along on Tony's trip to Brighton. She torments Tony on the trip and creates public scenes by making him look like a monster.

Themes

The Emptiness of Modern Life

A Handful of Dust is at heart a scathing indictment of modern, consumer-oriented life. Waugh is savage in his treatment of characters, including Polly Cockpurse and Brenda Last, who seek only pleasure in life without recognizing the role of morality, discipline, and sacrifice. With the expansion of industry in the early twentieth century, the prices of many consumer goods fell sharply. At the same time, new venues of entertainment, including the radio and the cinema, opened up a world of fun for those who had the resources. And it is fun that Brenda and her group of friends seek. Waugh portrays them as shallow and lacking any true interest in each other. When Brenda's relationship with Beaver falters and Tony leaves her without much money, her group moves on in search of the new "it girl" of the season. Waugh pointedly shows that none of these characters seems to truly enjoy themselves or gain anything lasting out of their modern, urban, materialistic lifestyles.

The Folly of Self-determination

Between 1900 and the outbreak of World War II, new forms of popular culture began to promise Britons that life was what you made it. Despite this growing power of optimistic imagery from advertising, film, and other forms of rhetoric seeking to convince people they could control the outcome of their lives, Evelyn Waugh had no faith in the power of self-determination. In his mind, human beings were largely corrupt and separated from God while the modern belief that most people were mostly good was delusional. Since only God could determine the outcome of a life, people should not strive to "recreate" themselves. In fact, doing so was a form of rejection of God's design. This is clearly mirrored in *A Handful of Dust* through the plot as a whole as well in the experiences of most of the central characters. Any attempt at liberation from social bonds, such as Brenda's affair and her flat in London, or Tony's dream of recreating a gothic fantasy world, end in failure. This is also true of John Beaver's wish to be socially popular, Jenny's desire to be exotic and interesting, and Dr. Messinger's hope of becoming a scientist who understands Indians. In the end, Waugh seems to argue, people's identities are determined, and those who try to radically alter their public personas are bound to be disappointed.

Topics for Further Study

- Research the ways in which Evelyn Waugh used his own experiences, especially the collapse of his first marriage, as inspiration for *A Handful of Dust*. What did he change? How did he elaborate on his experiences and what did he do to disguise or reveal the characters of the people involved? Write a paper looking at the choices Waugh made as an author in order to use his personal suffering as a way of investigating larger ideas.
- The novels of Charles Dickens play a large role in *A Handful of Dust*. Using guides such as this one, look at the story lines of the novels Tony read to Mr. Todd. Lead a class

discussion on Waugh's ambitions as a writer in the English tradition, focusing on the differences and similarities between *A Handful of Dust* and the novels of Dickens.

- Watch the 1988 film version of *A Handful of Dust* and prepare a video report for your class. Showing key scenes, discuss the ways in which the director, Charles Sturridge, adapted and perhaps condensed the novel. What did he leave out or add? Why do you suppose he made these choices? Were they successful?
- Waugh spends no effort in developing the characters in *A Handful of Dust* who are either servants or people of color. John's nanny, for example, is not even given a name. She is simply called "Nanny." Likewise, with the exception of Rosa, the people who guide Tony and Dr. Messinger are never named and hardly described, as if they were not important. Using your library and the Internet, research relations between classes and races in 1930s England and write a three-page paper showing how these prejudices are portrayed in the book.

The Uselessness of Nostalgia

History plays a central role in *A Handful of Dust*, in large part because of the rapidly changing nature of English society. Between the year of Waugh's birth and the publication of *A Handful of Dust* in 1934, England fought a devastating warm which decimated a generation of young men and crippled the nation's ability to hold on to its sprawling and expensive global empire. Thus, while the United States emerged from World War I with a booming economy and a new sense of global power, many in England came to believe that their nation's glory days were past. Many Britons took a reactionary stance against modern, socialistic England and had a nostalgic fondness for the bygone Victorian age of clear-cut social roles and expanding global power. Tony Last embodies this view, and from his introduction in the second chapter until his final hallucination in the jungle, he looks longingly back at a romanticized past, hoping somehow to be touched by its glory. Thus the names of the bedrooms at Hetton are from Arthurian legend. This is also why he prizes Hetton itself, remade in 1864, and why he enjoys the literally Victorian sermons of Reverend Tendril. Even his escape from Brenda into the jungles of South America is a search for a lost city of the past, a passageway out of the present. It is not by chance that Tony's view of "the City" is not South American but rather resembles a medieval castle. In effect, this nostalgia paralyzes Tony, making him unable to either participate in the contemporary world or to find a viable alternative to it. Waugh did not share his hero's nostalgia, however, at least not for the solidity of the Victorian age. As Tony's experience shows, for Waugh, nostalgia was another force separating people from the true nature of their lives.

Style

Irony

Waugh uses irony to create the collapsing world of the Lasts in *A Handful of Dust*. Irony as a literary style is a way authors can use words to bring out a meaning separate from the ones the actual words convey. Often, the intended meaning is the opposite of the meaning of the words, such as when Brenda writes Tony a note to tell him she loves John Beaver and signs it, "Best love from Brenda." Clearly, Waugh's intended meaning is not that Brenda is giving Tony her best love. Another example is when Waugh notes that Tony "had got into the habit of loving and trusting Brenda," the actual meaning of the sentence is that Tony is blind to the fact that his wife has been openly cheating on him. Or, to cite another example, when Brenda complains to Tony that "Everything has been so difficult," Waugh's intention is to show how selfish Brenda is, not how hard a time she has had after leaving Tony. Thus, by using irony, Waugh allows his characters to speak for themselves, to reveal their true selves through their unguarded words and feelings. This style is pleasing because it releases Waugh from having to comment on the action of the novel and keeps the narrator from hovering over every conversation. It also highlights the farcical nature of both Tony's failing marriage and the broader culture of narcissism.

The Hero's Journey

As identified by the scholar of mythology Joseph Campbell, Western literature is filled with heroes who leave home as young men, face a challenge or a danger, and return home transformed by the experience. Tony Last is clearly the hero of *A Handful of Dust*, but he far from overcomes his challenges. Like the classical hero he leaves home, though he is not altogether blameless for his situation. His journey is one into delusion rather than one of revelation. However, he is searching for the very myth that he had sustained at Hetton. Only late in his journey does he realize that "the City" does not exist. *A Handful of Dust* is in some ways a classical tragedy: Tony's fatal flaw is his inability to see the world as it is and his delusion is ultimately fatal.

Historical Context

The Great Depression

In Great Britain, the Great Depression, also known as the Great Slump, caused economic and social unrest throughout the early 1930s. Waugh makes reference to the Slump early in the novel. In the introduction of the character John Beaver, Waugh notes that since the Slump began "no one had been able to find anything for him to do." Unlike in the United States, where the economy in the 1920s boomed on a spree of speculation and credit, the British economy had struggled to recover from World War I. Throughout the 1920s exports suffered and unemployment was high. In 1926, a general strike spread from the coal mines through British industry, resulting in widespread clashes between strikers and the police. As a result of these factors as well as the crash of the American stock market in 1929, a national government was formed in 1930, comprised of representatives from the three major parties, the Liberals, Labour, and the Conservatives. Still, the economy struggled to regain its status as the world's most powerful. At the same time, England's hold on many of its colonies slipped, even as the ultra-nationalist Hitler took power in Germany (in 1933, the year before *A Handful of Dust* was published) and as Italy, led by the Italian fascist Benito Mussolini, invaded Ethiopia in 1935. At first, the government responded with measures that arguably made the Slump worse, including lowering benefits paid to unemployed workers and raising the income tax. By the mid-1930s, however, stimulating measures, such as the government-sponsored construction of millions of homes, helped the economy rebound. For those less affected by the economic downturn, the 1930s proved to be an exciting decade with the introduction of sound cinema, radios, vacuum cleaners, and washing machines. This is the world of expanded opportunities for consumerism in which Brenda and her circle move, mostly untouched by the economic downturn. By the late 1930s, preparations for war with Nazi Germany invigorated the British economy as industry retooled along military lines. Thus, the coming war, one which would again ultimately hurt the British economy, ironically helped Britain emerge from the Great Depression.

Compare & Contrast

- **1930s**: In England and the United States, a married person who seeks a divorce is compelled to prove unreasonable behavior on the part of their spouse and then wait a lengthy period for the government to finalize the divorce. When couples share a desire to end an unhappy marriage in which there has been no abuse or infidelity, they are often compelled to fabricate an affair, such as Tony Last does in *A Handful of Dust*.

Today: Although the United States began adopting so-called "no fault" divorce laws in the 1960s, the United Kingdom continues to offer only "fault divorce." Briefly, in the 1990s, reform advocates managed to pass legislation introducing a law under which couples could quickly end marriages, but it was rejected by the government. Today, it continues to take between two and five years to obtain a divorce in Great Britain.

- **1930s**: With no national system of roads and highways, travel by automobile between cities and towns was time-consuming and often frustrating. Most travel of more than a few miles was conducted by rail or, often in the case of freight, canals. In the late 1930s, a few years after the publication of *A Handful of Dust* the Ministry of Transport began a centrally planned Motorway system. This plan was shelved, however, because of World War II.

  Today: Great Britain is crisscrossed by a national Motorway system. Beginning with the opening of the Preston Bypass in the late 1950s, the Motorways were a response to the increasing popularity of automobile travel. Today, 2,200 miles of motorway serve some 28 million British cars. Train travel remains popular as well. Although travel by rail lost popularity between World War II and the 1980s, it has almost regained its highest historical levels of ridership.

- **1930s**: Great Britain continues to hold on to a number of Central and South American colonies, including British Honduras, British Guiana, the Faulkland Islands, Jamaica, the Bahamas, and Trinidad and Tobago. British control of the Caribbean is especially extensive. It is through many of these colonies that Tony travels on his quest for "the City."

  Today: Except for the Faulkland Islands, over which the United Kingdom fought a war with Argentina in the 1980s, all British colonies in South America have been granted independence or, in the case of the Mosquito Coast, have become divided up among neighboring countries. A handful of Caribbean islands remain under British control, including Turks and Caicos, Montserrat, and the British Virgin Islands.

English Fascism

As capitalism suffered during the Great Slump, a new political movement appeared in England, one which attracted many among the aristocracy. Founded by Sir Oswald Mosley in the early 1930s, the British Union of Fascists (BUF) was an authoritarian party on the political far right. Mosley, who had formerly represented first the Conservative Party and then the Labour Party as a member of Parliament, formed the group after a visit to fascist-ruled Italy in 1932. The BUF was completely top-down in structure, with Mosley himself the unquestioned leader of the movement. It is difficult to know how many members the BUF actually had, but the success of fascism in Italy and, after 1933, in Germany, caused many to take it more seriously than its actual size might have deserved. Still, the BUF staged several impressive mass rallies that resembled Nazi rallies in their use of spectacle. After Hitler's rise to power, Mosley also became more openly anti-Semitic, claiming Jews in Britain were all essentially foreigners and should be viewed with suspicion. He also called for increased royal power and a concentration of industry in a high commission, run by a prime minister to be appointed by the king. Eventually, Mosley would be incarcerated for the duration of World War II, and the fascist movement in Britain would collapse.

However, in the 1930s, many aristocrats and conservative intellectuals, including Evelyn Waugh and some notable heads of British corporations, were sympathetic to Franco in Spain, Mussolini in Italy, or, as in the case of King Edward VIII himself, Hitler in Germany. In fact, some historians have argued that Edward's wife, the American Wallace Simpson, in fact passed important secrets to the Nazis. Evelyn Waugh was friendly with Mosley and his wife, Diana Mitford Guinness Mosley. In fact, in 1930 Waugh dedicated his novel, *Vile Bodies*, to her. Waugh's feelings about fascism were complex. His approval of the Mussolini regime in Italy was colored in large part by his desire to support the policy of the Catholic Church. Initially, many English Catholics perceived Mussolini as a protector against Hitler's threat to Catholics, especially in Austria. Waugh's fondness changed in the late 1930s when Mussolini aligned himself with Hitler and began his own racist policies. For most Britons sympathetic to fascism, any positive feeling was snuffed out when war broke out in 1939.

Critical Overview

When *A Handful of Dust* appeared in 1934, Evelyn Waugh was already a writer well known for his satirical novels about the upper classes. Some reviewers saw *A Handful of Dust* as a continuation of this trend, though others perceived it to be more openly religious in tone. According to biographer Christopher Sykes, "When the book came out in 1934 the general opinion of Evelyn's public and critics was that he had written his best book to date." The Catholic periodical *The Tablet,* however, published a highly critical review, arguing that the book failed to represent Catholic ideals. Over time, however, it has come to be regarded as Waugh's finest work. Writing in the 1950s, the renowned critic Northrup Frye elevates Tony Last's plight to classical terms, calling it "close to a parody of tragic irony." In recent decades, critics have almost unanimously favored *A Handful of Dust* over Waugh's most famous work, *Brideshead Revisited.* Writing in the early 1990s, Frederick L. Beaty applauds Waugh's ability to simultaneously parody both the materialistic characters like Mrs. Beaver and Brenda Last as well as the powerless romantic Tony Last. "Indeed Waugh's outstanding success as an ironist in *A Handful of Dust* owes much to his ability to challenge the assumptions of both commercial and chivalric codes." Beaty points out that the novel does not preach. Rather, it argues through negative examples. "By showing the disorder wrought through living according to either instinct or hollow tradition, the novel demonstrates … the need for something higher than man-made ideals." David Wykes, in his 1999 book, *Evelyn Waugh: A literary Life,* summarizes the enthusiasm of most current critics of Waugh's work when he calls *A Handful of Dust* "Waugh's greatest single achievement."

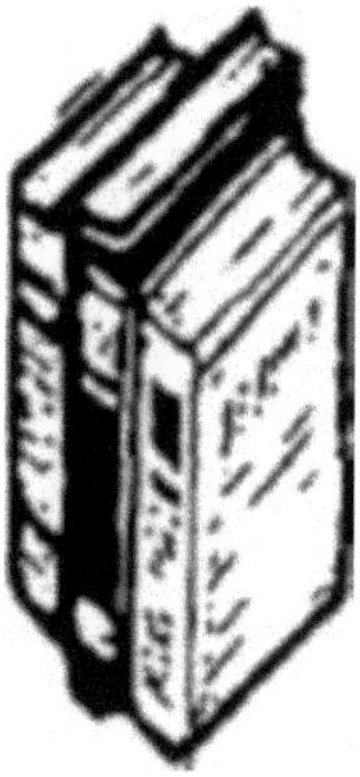

What Do I Read Next?

- D. J. Taylor's *Bright Young People: The Lost Generation of London's Jazz Age,* published in 2009, is a history of the social circle Evelyn Waugh cavorted with in 1920s London. Full of anecdotes and gossip about the "Bright Young Things," this book offers ample historical background to the action of *A Handful of Dust*.

- *Vile Bodies,* published in 1930, is Evelyn Waugh's second novel and, like *A Handful of Dust,* it parodies upper-class customs. In this case, the setting is the 1910s, on the eve of World War I. Like *A Handful of Dust, Vile Bodies* has a dramatic change of setting and tone in the second half of the novel as the hero, Adam Fenwick-Symes, is thrust into the war.
- *Brideshead Revisited,* which was published in 1945, is Waugh's most famous novel. It is much more overtly religious than *A Handful of Dust* and focuses much more squarely on the attraction of Catholicism to Britons in the years between the wars. It is also much more nostalgic, in large part because of the disruptions of life in Britain caused by World War II. It is *Brideshead Revisited,* and not the earlier, comedic novels, which made Waugh a literary figure in the United States.
- Novelist Graham Greene was a good friend of Evelyn Waugh's in large part because both men were converts to Catholicism. In 1951, Greene published his own novel on infidelity and religion, *The End of*

the Affair.

- Zora Neale Hurston's novel, *Their Eyes Were Watching God,* published in 1937, is the story of a poor African-American's three marriages in the U.S. South of the early twentieth century. The main character, Janie Crawford, is a fascinating contrast to Brenda Last and provides insight into how race and class affect people's ideas about marriage and love.

Sources

Beaty, Frederick L., "A Handful of Dust," in *The Ironic World of Evelyn Waugh: A Study of Eight Novels,* Northern Illinois University Press, 1992, pp. 86, 90, 110.

Frye, Northrup, "Historical Criticism: History of Modes," in *The Ironic World of Evelyn Waugh: A Study of Eight Novels,* edited by Frederick L. Beaty, Northern Illinois University Press, 1992, pp. 86-87; originally published in *Anatomy of Criticism,* Princeton University Press, 1957, p. 48.

Lane, Calvin W., "Chapter 1: The Artist and His World," in *Evelyn Waugh,* Twayne's English Author Series, No. 301, Twayne Publishers, 1981, p. 42.

Oldmeadow, Ernest, Review of *A Handful of Dust,* in *Evelyn Waugh: A Biography,* by Christopher Sykes, Little Brown and Co., 1975, pp. 140-41; originally published in *The Tablet,* September 8, 1934.

Patey, Douglas Lane, "Political Decade I (1930-1935)," in *The Life of Evelyn Waugh: A Critical Biography,* Blackwell Publishers, 1998, pp. 119, 123.

Sykes, Christopher, "1932-1934," in *Evelyn Waugh: A Biography,* Little, Brown, and Co., 1975, p. 140.

Waugh, Evelyn, *A Handful of Dust,* Back Bay Books, 1999 (1934).

Wykes, David, "Introduction," and "1930-1939," in *Evelyn Waugh: A Literary Life,* St. Martin's Press, 1999, pp. 8, 9, 103.

Further Reading

Kennedy, Dane, *Britain and Empire: 1880-1945,* Longman, 2002.

> This survey of British imperial history is a great introduction to the ways in which the empire affected people in the colonies as well as in Britain itself.

Lovell, Mary S., *The Sisters: The Saga of the Mitford Family,* W.W. Norton and Co., 2003.

> This history of the glamorous and scandalous Mitford sisters sheds light on the world in which Evelyn Waugh lived. Nancy was a friend of Waugh and a novelist; Unity was a close friend of Hitler; Diana was the wife of the leader of the British fascists.

Orwell, George, *The Road to Wigan Pier,* Mariner Books, 1972.

> Originally appearing in 1937, this book is one-half a report on the miserable conditions of the English working class during the Great Depression, and one-half an essay on the role of socialism in making conditions better.

Waugh, Alexander, *Fathers and Sons: The*

Biography of a Family, Anchor, 2008.

The grandson of Evelyn Waugh traces four generations of tension between fathers and sons in his famous family. Beginning with his great-grandfather, the publisher and critic Arthur Waugh, this book looks at the lives of the often unhappy, yet undeniably brilliant men of the Waugh family.

Milton Keynes UK
Ingram Content Group UK Ltd.
UKHW021053200324
439767UK00015B/462

GALE
CENGAGE Learning

Poetry for Students, Volume 9

Staff

Series Editors: Mary Ruby and Ira Mark Milne.

Contributing Editors: Elizabeth Bellalouna, Elizabeth Boden-miller, Angela Y. Jones, Michael L. LaBlanc, Polly Rapp.

Managing Editor: Dwayne D. Hayes.

Research: Victoria B. Cariappa, *Research Team Manager*. Cheryl Warnock, *Research Specialist*. Corrine A. Boland, Tamara Nott, Tracie A. Richardson, *Research Associates*. Timothy Lehnerer, Patricia Love, *Research Assistants*.

Permissions: Maria Franklin, *Permissions Manager*. Margaret A. Chamberlain, Edna Hedblad, *Permissions Specialists*. Erin Bealmear, *Permissions Associate*. Sandra K. Gore, *Permissions Assistant*.

Production: Mary Beth Trimper, *Production*

Director. Evi Seoud, *Assistant Production Manager*. Stacy Melson, *Production Assistant*.

Imaging and Multimedia Content Team: Randy Bassett, *Image Database Supervisor*. Robert Duncan, *Imaging Specialist*. Michael Logusz, *Graphic Artist*. Pamela A. Reed, *Imaging Coordinator*. Dean Dauphinais, Robyn V. Young, *Senior Image Editors*. Kelly A. Quin, *Image Editor*

Product Design Team: Cynthia Baldwin, *Product Design Manager*. Pamela A. E. Galbreath, *Senior Art Director*. Gary Leach, *Graphic Artist*.

Copyright Notice

Since this page cannot legibly accommodate all copyright notices, the acknowledgments constitute an extension of the copyright notice.

While every effort has been made to secure permission to reprint material and to ensure the reliability of the information presented in this publication, Gale Research neither guarantees the accuracy of the data contained herein nor assumes any responsibility for errors, omissions, or discrepancies. Gale accepts no payment for listing; and inclusion in the publication of any organization, agency, institution, publication, service, or individual does not imply endorsement of the editors or publisher. Errors brought to the attention of the publisher and verified to the satisfaction of the publisher will be corrected in future editions.

This publication is a creative work fully protected by all applicable copyright laws, as well as by misappropriation, trade secret, unfair competition, and other applicable laws. The authors and editors of this work have added value to the underlying factual material herein through one or more of the following: unique and original selection, coordination, expression, arrangement, and classification of the information. All rights to this publication will be vigorously defended.

Copyright © 2000
The Gale Group
27500 Drake Rd.
Farmington Hills, MI 48331-3535

All rights reserved including the right of reproduction in whole or in part in any form.

ISBN 0-7876-3570-7
ISSN 1094-7019

Printed in the United States of America.
10 9 8 7 6 5 4 3 2 1

Elegy Written in a Country Churchyard

Thomas Gray 1751

Introduction

Thomas Gray's "Elegy Written in a Country Churchyard" was first published in 1751. Gray may, however, have begun writing the poem in 1742, shortly after the death of his close friend Richard West. An elegy is a poem which laments the dead. Gray's "Elegy Written in a Country Churchyard" is noteworthy in that it mourns the death not of great or famous people, but of common men. The speaker of this poem sees a country churchyard at sunset, which impels him to meditate on the nature of human mortality. The poem invokes the classical idea of *memento mori,* a Latin phrase which states plainly to all mankind, "Remember that you must die." The speaker considers the fact that in death, there is no difference between great and common people. He goes on to wonder if among the lowly people buried in the churchyard there had been any natural poets or politicians whose talent had simply never been discovered or nurtured. This thought leads him to praise the dead for the honest, simple lives that they lived.

Gray did not produce a great deal of poetry; the "Elegy Written in a Country Churchyard," however, has earned him a respected and deserved place in literary history. The poem was written at the end of the Augustan Age and at the beginning of the Romantic period, and the poem has characteristics associated with both literary periods. On the one hand, it has the ordered, balanced phrasing and rational sentiments of Neoclassical poetry. On the other hand, it tends toward the emotionalism and individualism of the Romantic poets; most importantly, it idealizes and elevates the common man.

Author Biography

Born in the Cornhill district of London in 1716, Gray was the son of Dorothy Antrobus Gray, a milliner, and Philip Gray, a scrivener. Gray's father was a mentally disturbed and violent man who at times abused his wife. Gray attended Eton School from 1725 until 1734, when he entered Cambridge University. He left Cambridge in 1738 without taking a degree, intending to study law in London. However, he and childhood friend Horace Walpole embarked on an extended tour of Europe. The two separated in Italy in 1741 after a quarrel, and Gray continued the journey on his own. He returned to London later in the year, shortly before his father died. Gray then moved with his mother to Stoke Poges, Buckinhamshire, and began his most productive period of poetic composition. In 1742 Grey wrote his first major poem, "Ode on the Spring," which he sent to his close friend Richard West—unknowingly on the very day of West's death from tuberculosis. In the next three months Gray wrote "Ode on a Distant Prospect of Eton College," "Hymn to Adversity," and "Sonnet on the Death of Mr. Richard West." It is believed that he also worked on "Elegy Written in a Country Churchyard" during this time, though this poem was not published until 1751. Gray returned to Cambridge at the end of 1742 and received a Bachelor of Civil Law degree the next year. Gray lived at the university for most of the rest of his life, but he never took part in tutoring, lecturing, or other academic duties; instead he pursued his studies and writing, taking advantage of the intellectual stimulation of the setting. In 1757 Gray was offered the position of Poet Laureate, but he declined it. He moved to London in 1759 to study at the British Museum and remained there for two years. He read widely and earned a reputation as one of the most learned men in Europe. Except for regular trips back to London and elsewhere in England, Gray stayed in Cambridge from 1761 until the end of his life. In 1768 Gray was named Regius Professor of Modern History at Cambridge, an office he held until his death in 1771.

Poem Summary

Lines 1-4

In the first stanza, the speaker observes the signs of a country day drawing to a close: a curfew bell ringing, a herd of cattle moving across the pasture, and a farm laborer returning home. The speaker is then left alone to contemplate the isolated rural scene. The first line of the poem sets a distinctly somber tone: the curfew bell does not simply ring; it "knells"—a term usually applied to bells rung at a death or funeral. From the start, then, Gray reminds us of human mortality.

Lines 5-8

The second stanza sustains the somber tone of the first: the speaker is not mournful, but pensive, as he describes the peaceful landscape that surrounds him. Even the air is characterized as having a "solemn stillness."

Lines 9-12

The sound of an owl hooting intrudes upon the evening quiet. We are told that the owl "complains"; in this context, the word does not mean "to whine" or "grumble," but "to express sorrow." The owl's call, then, is suggestive of grief.

Note that at no point in these three opening stanzas does Gray directly refer to death or a funeral; rather, he indirectly creates a funereal atmosphere by describing just a few mournful sounds.

Lines 13-16

It is in the fourth stanza that the speaker directly draws our attention to the graves in the country churchyard. We are presented with two potentially conflicting images of death. Line 14 describes the heaps of earth surrounding the graves; in order to dig a grave, the earth must necessarily be disrupted. Note that the syntax of this line is slightly confusing. We would expect this sentence to read "Where the turf heaves"—not "where heaves the turf": Gray has inverted the word order. Just as the earth has been disrupted, the syntax imitates the way in which the earth has been disrupted. But by the same token, the "rude Forefathers" buried beneath the earth seem entirely at peace: we are told that they are laid in "cells," a term which reminds us of the quiet of a monastery, and that they "sleep."

Lines 17-20

If the "Forefathers" are sleeping, however, the speaker reminds us that they will never again rise from their "beds" to hear the pleasurable sounds of country life that the living do. The term "lowly beds" describes not only the unpretentious graves in which the forefathers are buried, but the humble conditions that they endured when they were alive.

Media Adaptations

- J. Norton Publishers/Audio-Forum has produced an audiocassette entitled *How Shelley Died; Elegy in a Country Churchyard: Two Lectures* (1979) with Gilbert Highet.
- Caedmon has produced an audiocassette set (of 4 disks) entitled *Eighteenth Century Poets and Drama* (1970).
- Spoken Arts Corporation has produced an audiocassette set (of 6 disks) entitled *Great English Literature of the 18th Century* (1971).
- Perspective Films has produced a videocassette entitled *Elegy to Thomas Gray* (1980).

- Monterey Home Video has produced a videocassette entitled *The Poetry Hall of Fame: Volume IV* (1994) from the BBC series "Anyone for Tennyson?"

Lines 21-24

The speaker then moves on to consider some of the other pleasures the dead will no longer enjoy: the happiness of home, wife, and children.

Lines 25-28

The dead will also no longer be able to enjoy the pleasures of work, of plowing the fields each day. This stanza points to the way in which the "Elegy Written in a Country Churchyard" contains elements of both Augustan and Romantic poetry. Poetry that describes agriculture—as this one does —is called georgic. Georgic verse was extremely popular in the eighteenth century. Note, however, that Gray closely identifies the farmers with the land that they work. This association of man and nature is suggestive of a romantic attitude. The georgic elements of the stanza almost demand that we characterize it as typical of the eighteenth century, but its tone looks forward to the Romantic period.

Lines 29-32

The next four stanzas caution those who are wealthy and powerful not to look down on the poor. These lines warn the reader not to slight the “obscure” “destiny” of the poor—the fact that they will never be famous or have long histories, or “annals,” written about them.

Lines 33-36

This stanza invokes the idea of *memento mori* (literally, a reminder of mortality). The speaker reminds the reader that regardless of social position, beauty, or wealth, all must eventually die.

Lines 37-40

The speaker also challenges the reader not to look down on the poor for having modest, simple graves. He suggests, moreover, that the elaborate memorials that adorn the graves of the “Proud” are somehow excessive. In this context, the word “fretted” in line 39 has a double meaning: on the one hand, it can refer to the design on a cathedral ceiling; on the other hand, it can suggest that there is something “fretful,” or troublesome, about the extravagant memorials of the wealthy.

Lines 41-44

The speaker observes that nothing can bring the dead back to life, and that all the advantages that the wealthy had in life are useless in the face of death. Neither elaborate funeral monuments nor impressive honors can restore life. Nor can flattery in some way be used to change the mind of death. Note here Gray's use of personification in characterizing both "flattery" and "death"—as though death has a will or mind of its own.

Lines 45-48

The speaker then reconsiders the poor people buried in the churchyard. He wonders what great deeds they might have accomplished had they been given the opportunity: one of these poor farmers, the speaker reasons, might have been a great emperor; another might have "waked … the living lyre," or been a great poet or musician.

Lines 49-52

The poor were never able to fulfill their political and artistic potential, however, because they were uneducated—they never received the "Knowledge" that would enable them to rule and to create. Instead, "Penury," or poverty, "froze the genial current of their soul." That is, poverty paralyzed their ability to draw upon their innermost passions—the very passions that could have inspired them to become great poets or politicians.

Lines 53-56

In a series of analogies, Gray observes that the talents of the poor are like a "gem" hidden in the ocean or a "flower" blooming in the desert. Just as an unseen flower in the desert is a "waste," Gray suggests, the uneducated talents of the poor are also a "waste," because they remain unused and undeveloped.

Lines 57-60

The speaker then compares these poor, uneducated people to three of the most famous and powerful people of the previous century: John Hampden, a parliamentary leader who defended the people against the abuses of Charles I; John Milton, the great poet who wrote *Paradise Lost* and who also opposed Charles I; and Oliver Cromwell, Lord Protector of England from 1653 to 1658. The speaker suggests that buried in this churchyard might be someone who—like Hampden, Milton, or Cromwell—had the innate ability to oppose tyranny, but never had the opportunity to exercise that ability.

Lines 61-64

This person, the speaker reasons, with the proper education and resources, might have "commanded" the government as well as any great political leader. Note, however, that Gray gives us two ways in which to consider this power. On the one hand, a great ruler can receive applause and can ignore "threats of pain and ruin." A great leader can "scatter plenty," can offer prosperity, to a grateful nation. But on the other hand, if one governs, one is, in fact, exposed to dangerous threats. And simply governing to receive “applause” suggests a shallow and self-serving motive. Moreover, “scattering plenty” implies that the wealth of a nation can be squandered by its rulers. Gray may be suggesting that having power is not as desirable as it seems. Note that the final line of this stanza is enjambed; it continues into the following line—and in this case, the next stanza.

Lines 65-68

The first line of this stanza continues the thought of the previous, enjambed line. It abruptly reminds us that the impoverished conditions of the poor “forbade” them from becoming great rulers. Gray underscores the abrupt shock of this idea by abruptly interrupting the flow of the line with a caesura. Building on the idea of the previous stanza, the speaker notes that if poverty prevented the country laborers from acquiring the “virtues” of great and powerful people, it also prevented them from committing the “crimes” often associated with those people—and especially with those people who hold political power. In particular, it prevented them from engaging in the bloody activity associated with the British Civil War.

Lines 69-72

Because these farm laborers were not in positions of power, the speaker reasons, they never had to ignore their own consciences. Nor did they sacrifice their artistic talents (the gift of the “Muse”) to “Luxury” or “Pride.”

Lines 73-76

The speaker continues his praise of the simple life of common people. They are “far from the madding crowd” of city and political life. “Madding” here can mean either “maddening” (that is, the source of madness or insanity) or it can mean “mad” (that is, the crowd is itself hatefully insane). In either case, the common country people were removed from this insane world; as a result, they never “strayed” into the immoral acts of the powerful. Instead, they kept steadily to their simple but meaningful lives.

Lines 77-80

The speaker then reminds us that these common people are, in fact, long dead. He notes that even if they were not powerful or great, and even if they do not have an elaborate memorial of the sort mentioned in line 38, they still deserve homage or tribute. At the very least, he suggests, an onlooker should “sigh” on seeing their graves. Note here the multiple meanings we can attach to the word “passing.” It can refer to the onlooker, who is simply walking or “passing by” these graves. It can mean “in passing”—that someone seeing these graves should take just a moment out of their busy lives to remember the dead. And “passing” itself is a euphemism for death. In a way, then, Gray is suggesting that there is no difference between the person "passing" by the grave and the person who has "passed" away—another reminder that all will eventually die.

Lines 81-84

Instead of "fame and elegy," the people buried here have modest tombstones, which display only their names and the dates of their birth and death. These common people were not famous, and no one has written elaborate elegies or funeral verses for them. Still, the very modesty of their tombstones testifies to the nobility and "holy" nature of their simple lives. As such, they provide an example not so much of how life should be lived, but how its end, death, should be approached. The term "rustic moralist" here is open to interpretation. It may refer to anyone who is in the countryside thinking about the meaning of death. But more likely, it refers to the speaker, who is himself moralizing—preaching or contemplating—about the nature of both life and death.

Lines 85-88

The speaker reasons that most people, faced with the prospect of dying and ultimately being forgotten, cling to life. Note Gray's use of paradox in line 86: "this pleasing anxious being." On the one hand, "being" or living can be "anxious," filled with worries. On the other hand, just being alive— when faced with death—is itself "pleasing" or pleasant. The speaker is suggesting that even the troubles and worries of life are enjoyable in comparison to death.

Lines 89-92

The dead rely on the living to remember them and to mourn for them. The speaker suggests that this need is so fundamental that even from the grave the buried dead seem to ask for remembrance. In fact, as line 92 suggests, the dead actually live on in our memories.

Lines 93-96

In this stanza, the speaker addresses himself. He reasons that since he himself has been mindful of the dead, and has remembered and praised them in this poem, perhaps when he is dead someone will remember him. This person, he reasons, will necessarily be a "kindred Spirit," someone who is also a lonely wanderer in the country, meditating on the nature of death. The speaker then goes on to imagine his own death: he envisions this "kindred Spirit" seeing his (the speaker's) grave and wondering about his life and death.

Lines 97-100

In the next five stanzas, the speaker imagines how an old farm laborer might remember him after his death. If, the speaker speculates, the "kindred Spirit" sees the speaker's grave and wonders about it, perhaps an old man might offer to describe the speaker. The old man would say that the speaker was often seen wandering about the countryside at dawn. Presumably, he was frequently out all night —as, no doubt, he has been in this very poem.

Lines 101-104

At noon, the old man continues, the speaker would frequently stretch out under an old tree at noon, and stare at a nearby brook.

Lines 105-108

The old man would have observed that the speaker's moods were changeable: sometimes the speaker would wander about in the nearby woods, "smiling scornfully" and talking to himself; other times, he would appear depressed; then again, sometimes he would look as though he were in anguish. Perhaps, the old man speculates, the speaker had been "crossed in hopeless love."

Lines 109-112

The speaker continues to imagine this old man remembering him after his death. The old man would have noticed one morning that the speaker was absent: he was not in any of his favorite spots. Likewise, the old man would remember, the speaker did not appear the following day.

Lines 113-116

The third day, however, the old man and his

friends would have seen the speaker's body being carried to the churchyard for burial. (The speaker, then, is imagining himself buried in the very graveyard he once used to wander by.) The old man invites this curious passerby, or "kindred Spirit," to read the speaker's epitaph. Note the reminder that the old man is uneducated: he cannot read, although the passerby can do so.

Lines 117-120

The last three stanzas are, in fact, the speaker's epitaph; the way in which the speaker imagines his epitaph will read. Through the epitaph, the speaker asks the passerby (and the reader) not to remember him as wealthy, famous, or brilliantly educated, but as one who was "melancholic" or deeply thoughtful and sad.

Lines 121-124

The speaker asks that we remember him for being generous and sincere. His generosity was, in fact, his willingness to mourn for the dead. Because he was so generous, the speaker reasons, heaven gave him a "friend"—someone who would, in turn, mourn for him after his death. This friend is unnamed, but we can deduce that it is any "kindred Spirit"—including the reader—who reads the speaker's epitaph and remembers him.

Lines 125-128

The speaker concludes by cautioning the reader not to praise him any further. He also asks that his "frailties," his flaws or personal weaknesses, not be considered; rather, they should be left to the care of God, with whom the speaker now resides. The poem, then, is an elegy not only for the common man, but for the speaker himself. Indeed, by the end of the poem it is evident that the speaker himself wishes to be identified not with the great and famous, but with the common people whom he has praised and with whom he will, presumably, be buried.

Themes

Death

Gray's "Elegy" is one of the best-known poems about death in all of European literature. The poem presents the reflections of an observer who, passing by a churchyard that is out in the country, stops for a moment to think about the significance of the strangers buried there. Scholars of medieval times sometimes kept human skulls on their desktops, to keep themselves conscious of the fact that someday they, like the skulls' former occupants, would die: from this practice we get the phrase *memento mori,* which we say to this day to describe any token one uses to keep one's mortality in mind. In this poem, the graveyard acts as a *memento mori,* reminding the narrator to not place too much value on this life because someday he too will be dead and buried. The speaker of the poem is surrounded by the idea of death, and throughout the first seven stanzas there are numerous images pointing out the contrast between death and life. After mentioning the churchyard in the title, which establishes the theme of mortality, the poem itself begins with images of gloom and finality. The darkness at the end of the day, the forlorn moan of lowing cattle, the stillness of the air (highlighted by the beetle's stilted motion) and the owl's nocturnal hooting all serve to set a background for this serious meditation. However, it is not until the fourth stanza that the poem actually begins to deal with the cemetery, mentioned as the place where the village forefathers "sleep." In the following stanzas, the speaker tries to imagine what the lives of these simple men might have been like, touching upon their relations with their wives, children, and the soil that they worked. They are not defined by their possessions, because they had few, and instead are defined by their actions, which serves to contrast their lives with their quiet existence in the graveyard. This "Elegy" presents the dead in the best light: their families adored them and they were cheerful in their work, as they "hummed the woods beneath their steady stroke." The speaker openly admits that they are spoken of so well precisely because they are dead, because death is such a terrible thing that its victims deserve the respect of the living. In line 90, the poet explains, "Some pious drops the closing eye requires," explaining that the living should show their respect for death with their sorrow.

Search for Self

The speaker of this poem goes through a process of recognizing what is important to him and choosing how to live his life (which leads to the epitaph with which he would like to be remembered). In stanza 8, the poem begins naming the attributes that are normally considered desirable but are now considered pointless when compared with the lives of the rustic dead in the country graveyard. Ambition and Grandeur, according to the speaker, should not think less of these people because of their simple accomplishments. He goes on to assert that Pride and Memory have no right to ignore them, and that Honor and Flattery will be as useless to the rich as to the poor when they are dead. The speaker, an educated person, gives much consideration to the subject of Knowledge, and whether the lack of it made the lives of these country people less significant. Their poverty blocked the way to knowledge, he decides, and the lack of knowledge separated them from vices as well as virtues, so that in the end he does not consider his education a factor in making him better or worse than them either. In the end, having eliminated all of the supposed benefits of the wealthy, educated world that he comes from, the speaker identifies himself with the graveyard inhabitants to such a degree that he winds up in this humble graveyard after his death. In contrast to the simple graves that he pondered over throughout his life, though, the speaker's grave is marked with a warm-hearted memorial, the "Epitaph" at the end of the poem. Assuming that such a thoughtful person would not have been so immodest as to write this epitaph for himself, there must have been some other literate person to remember him. He is also remembered by an illiterate member of the farm community, the "hoary-headed swain" who has to ask someone to read the epitaph. Before the death of the poem's narrator, this Swain established a nonverbal relationship with him, observing him from afar, wondering about him just as the narrator wondered about the country people buried there.

Topics for Further Study

- Do you think the speaker of this poem is sentimentalizing the forgotten people in the country churchyard, or is he giving them the recognition they deserve? Would this poem have the same meaning if it were written in a churchyard in a busy city?
- Visit a cemetery near you, pick the tombstone of a person that you do not know, and write a page about what that person might have been like, focusing on the social changes that person may have experienced. What does the length of that person's life tell you? What can you tell from where they are buried?
- It could be argued that people in

modern society are more likely to remember the accomplishments of poor people than they were in Gray's time? It is just as possible, though, that we are as preoccupied with the famous and wealthy as people in seventeenth century England were with royalty. Explain what you think about this issue.

Class Conflict

A superficial reading of this poem might leave the impression that the author intends to present members of the lower class as being more worthy of praise than their upper-class counterparts. This would be a reasonable assumption, since so much of the poem is devoted to praising the simple virtues of the poor. In the larger scope, though, the position that Gray takes is that all people, poor or rich, are equal. This is a meditation on death, which has been called the "great equalizer" because no can avoid it. The reason that the poem seems to favor one class over the other is that it is working against the assumption that only those of the upper class are worthy of attention when they die. It is the humble condition of the country churchyard, with gravestones unmarked or possibly marked just with names by illiterate people unable to read, that draws attention to the virtues of the poor and uneducated (which society often forgets), and so much of the poem is spent praising their moral strength. The virtues of the wealthy and famous are not denied, they just are not explored in this poem because they are already so familiar. Evidence of the poem's evenhandedness about the different classes can be seen in the fact that, while praising the poor country people throughout, Gray also acknowledges that education, which may give them opportunity to develop moral excellence, may also lead them to corruption: as he says in stanza 17, the humble circumstances of the poor limited the growth not only of their virtues but also of their crimes. The poem thus leaves open the question of superiority. Society glorifies the rich, and the poem's narrator glorifies the poor, but, as he reminds us, "The paths of glory lead but to the grave."

Style

"Elegy Written in a Country Churchyard" is written in heroic quatrains. A quatrain is a four-line stanza. Heroic quatrains rhyme in an *abab* pattern and are written in iambic pentameter. An iamb is a poetic foot consisting of one unstressed and one stressed syllable, as in the phrase "the world." Pentameter simply means that there are five feet in each line. Consider, for instance, the first line of Gray's "Elegy Written in a Country Churchyard": The Curfew tolls the knell of parting day.

When we scan the line, or identify its stresses, it appears as follows: TheCur *few tolls* the knell *of part* ing day.

Try reading the line aloud: its regular, steady rhythm helps to creates a calm and quiet mood—one appropriate to the meditative nature of this poem.

Historical Context

When Thomas Gray was writing this poem, the world was going through a period of intellectual development that thinkers of the time dubbed the "Age of Enlightenment." The Enlightenment was a philosophical movement that grew out of the great advances made by scientists in the seventeenth and eighteenth centuries. One key example which ended up having great influence on the Enlightenment was Sir Isaac Newton's theory of universal gravitation, which proposed laws that explained and predicted the behavior of matter in all circumstances everywhere. Newton published this theory in his book *Philosophiae Naturalis Principia Mathematica* in 1687, and it marked a turning point in the history of science. At the same time, this idea of the power of rationalism was growing in the area of philosophy. Thinkers such as Rene Descartes (1596-1650) and Baruch Spinoza (1632-1677) took up the idea of rationalism, attempting to apply the methods of scientific inquiry to the field of philosophy; Descartes' famous statement "I think, therefore I am" represents his attempt to start with the one simple truth that he could be sure of about the world, which was that he himself existed. In political science, Thomas Hobbes (1588-1679) explored the interrelations of social interactions in such works as *The Elements of Law, Natural and Politic,* and John Locke (1632-1704) explained human intelligence as being the sum of what is learned through experience, not the God-given right of a few.

By the start of the eighteenth century, intellectuals throughout the world were excited about the new Age of Enlightenment, which promised humanity new hope for controlling the world's problems. At first, though, the Enlightenment's enthusiasts were considered dangerous radicals. They rejected tradition that was not backed up with solid rational explanation, and tradition was the basis for most rulers' political power. Royalty ruled by relation to previous rulers, and landowners feasted while peasants starved because of rights based on inheritance, but rationalism served to undermine such rights and to blur class distinctions. In particular, the Catholic Church, which had been a strong influence in European politics for centuries, was threatened by the skepticism of Enlightenment thinkers who felt society should be organized according to rational rather than religious principles. As religious explanations of the universe lost credibility to scientific explanations that were based on observation, the Church took a defensive position, jailing free thinkers for heresy when they published theories that contradicted church tradition. In earlier times, Galileo, for example, was imprisoned for supporting the Copernican heliocentric view of the solar system. In the early 1700s, the church clashed frequently with Enlightenment theorists who made even minor claims about the nature of man and society that could be considered heretical. By the middle of the century, when Thomas Gray wrote his

"Elegy," Enlightenment rationality had gained enough public support to stand on its own. To some extent, the poem displays Enlightenment principles in the way that the speaker shows faith that the rural poor could be intelligent and successful if they had proper education, reflecting Locke's theory of the mind as a "blank slate" that is ready to grow. The pessimism he shows, though, regarding the potential for corruption if the poor were educated, is contrary to the standard Enlightenment optimism about the good that will result from education.

Compare & Contrast

- **1751:** Benjamin Franklin, flying a kite in a thunderstorm with a key at the end of the string, discovered the fact that lightning behaves like electricity and flows through conductive material.

  Today: Control of electricity is one of the fundamental principles of our society. Blackouts, when electricity becomes unavailable, create major disruptions.

- **1751:** Whaling was an important part of the economy of the New England colonies, with more than sixty whaling ships trolling the water off the coast.

  Today: Environmental

organizations fight to protect the rights of endangered whale species, but the world has much less use for whale meat or for whale oil to light lamps.

- **1751:** English theologian and evangelist John Wesley was travelling almost 5000 miles every year to spread the word about Christianity, founding the denomination known as Methodism.

  Today: Methodism is recognized as one of the mainstream Protestant religions.

- **1751:** Approximately one-fifth of the people in New England, which was to become America after the war for independence in 1776, were slaves.
  1863: Abraham Lincoln issued the Emancipation Proclamation, which made slavery illegal in the United States. It was not accepted in the South until after their defeat in the Civil War in 1865.

  Today: Most of the world has laws against slavery, but there are still regular scattered reports of people, usually immigrants and females, who are forced into labor against their wills.

- **1751:** Denis Diderot published the first volume of the first modern encyclopedia, his *Encyclopaedie, ou Dictionaire raisonne des sciences, des arts et des metiers, par une societe de gens de lettres*. The work eventually spanned eleven volumes, with the last volume finished in 1772.

  Today: Many established encyclopedias, as well as uncollected information that is compiled into encyclopedias, is available from a computer terminal from anywhere on the globe via the Internet.

The high point for the Enlightenment was the American Revolution in 1776. This marked the beginning of a society based on rationality and fairness, not tradition. The basis for the American Revolution was that people living in North America would now be better able to decide what was best for them than a king living in England, reflecting a faith in the common person's ability to reason. The Declaration of Independence is a major philosophical work concerning the rights of human beings to determine their own fates. The end of the Enlightenment as an intellectual movement came soon after, however, with the French Revolution from 1789 to 1799. Like the revolution in America, the French Revolution was an attempt to let individuals control their own destinies, based on faith in reason, which Enlightenment thinkers had been advocating for nearly a hundred years. While the American Revolution created a new society, however, the French Revolution created chaos, a bloodbath of government suppression of revolutionaries and public executions of deposed government figures. In the end, the oppressive system of feudal land ownership was abolished, but only at the end of a bitter struggle that required both sides to focus their attention on jingoistic slogans. The ideal of rationality became lost with the emphasis on the rights of individuals and the belief that the simple, uncorrupt poor know better than the pampered rich. The Enlightenment gave way to the age of Romanticism, which emphasized an almost mystical belief in individuality and the goodness of nature.

Critical Overview

Over the years, Gray's "Elegy Written in a Country Churchyard" has received extensive critical attention. Critics have long recognized Gray's "Elegy Written in a Country Churchyard" for its restrained and dignified expression of simple truths. In *Lives of the English Poets,* Samuel Johnson praised the poem for its universal appeal and its originality: "The 'Churchyard' abounds with images which find a mirrour in every mind, and with sentiments to which every bosom returns an echo are to me original.... Had Gray written often thus, it had been vain to blame, and useless to praise him." Other writers, such as Samuel Coleridge and Matthew Arnold, also admired the work, although Arnold's criticism was somewhat cautious. Arnold noted in his *Essays in Criticism* that "the 'Elegy Written in a Country Churchyard' is a beautiful poem ... But it is true that the 'Elegy Written in a Country Churchyard' owe[s] much of its success to its subject, and that it has received a too unmeasured and unbounded praise."

In the twentieth century, critics have often observed two competing "voices" or attitudes in Gray's writings. Joseph Wood Krutch, in his introduction to *The Selected Letters of Thomas Gray,* offers a useful comparison of the classical and Romantic tendencies in the "Elegy Written in a Country Churchyard." Krutch maintains that there are certainly strong romantic qualities in the poem, but that it is more clearly identifiable with the eighteenth century: "there is nothing mystical, at least nothing transcendental, in the 'Elegy Written in a Country Churchyard.' It is everywhere stubbornly rational, even in its melancholy. The simple life, even the life close to nature, is good because it is healthful and free from great temptation, not because God dwells in a sunset." In more recent years, critical attention has been focused on Gray's complex use of language. Some critics have noted a degree of ambiguity in Gray's syntax. One critic, W. Hutchings, argues in an essay in *Studies in Philology* that this ambiguity tends to "undermine" the apparently secure or simple universe that Gray has depicted. Hutchings notes, "there is an extraordinary degree of instability about [the 'Elegy Written in a Country Churchyard'], one which often expresses itself by making its syntax fluid, even indeterminate. Far from being something to be amended or ignored, this quality is the key to the 'Elegy Written in a Country Churchyard.'" We notice, then, a transformation in the way in which this poem has been viewed: early critics tended to praise the poem for its simple truths; more recent critics, however, have begun to wonder if underneath these apparently simple truths there are more troubling questions.

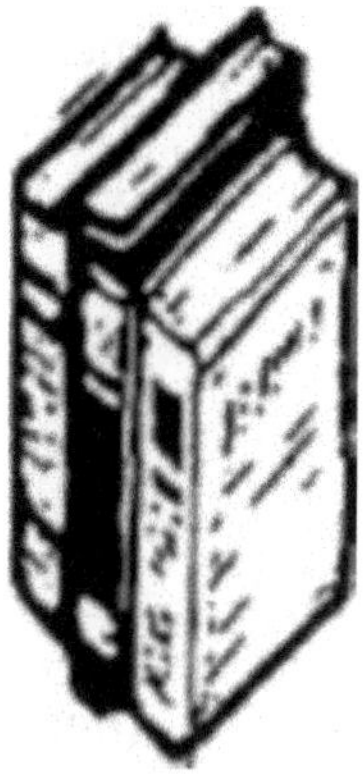

What Do I Read Next?

- The most authoritative edition of Gray's poetry is the edition originally published by the Oxford Press in 1966, entitled *The Complete Poems of Thomas Gray: English, Latin and Greek*. H. W. Starr wrote the introduction and edited the book with J. R. Hendrickson.
- John Dyer is a Welsh pastoral poet who wrote at the same time as Gray. His greatest works, including "Grongar Hill," considered one of the first romantic pastoral poems, are included in the collection *Poems, 1761*.
- Samuel Johnson was the outstanding literary figure of Gray's time. Among his writings was the ten-

volume *Lives of the Poets,* which includes a brief biography of Gray, as well as a number of poems that he wrote himself. He is best known today for the biography that James Boswell wrote about him, *The Life of Samuel Johnson,* considered one of the best biographies ever and an important source for readers who want to understand the British literary scene in the eighteenth century.

- Gray wrote during the Age of Enlightenment, a period of intense intellectual activity throughout the world. One of the leading thinkers of the time was French Philosopher Rene Descartes, who is often credited with adding humanity to the age of ideas. His *Discourse on Method and the Meditations* is still considered one of the world's most important philosophical works.
- Thomas Gray is often considered a poet ahead of his time, who predated the Romantic Movement that swept across the globe approximately fifty years later. More than his contemporaries, his contemplative style, and concern for humanity are often compared to the works of William Wordsworth, one of the

founders of Romanticism. Wordsworth's "Lines Composed A Few Miles Above Tintern Abbey, on Revisiting the Banks of the Wye During a Tour, July 13th, 1798," has a much looser structure than Gray's "Elegy," but there is a similarity in the melancholy of both poems.

- Richard Gough's *The History of Myddle* was written between 1700 and 1706, chronicling the lives of people living in the small English town of Myddle in Shropshire. This rural history is probably as close as one can get to reading about the lives of the people discussed in Gray's "Elegy." A 1980 edition of Gough's book is available, with an introduction by Dr. Peter Razzell.

Sources

Arnold, Matthew, "Thomas Gray," in his *Essays in Criticism,* 2nd ser., The Macmillan Company, 1934, pp. 69-99.

Brady, Frank, "Structure and Meaning in Gray's *Elegy,*" in *Thomas Gray's Elegy Written in a Country Churchyard,* edited by Harold Bloom, Philadelphia: Chelsea House Publishers, 1987.

Ellis, Frank Hale, "Gray's *Elegy:* The Biographical Problem in Literary Criticism," in *Twentieth Century Interpretations of Gray's "Elegy,"* edited by Herbert W. Starr, Englewood Cliffs, NJ: Prentice-Hall, Inc., 1968.

Empson, William, "Proletarian Literature," in *English Pastoral Poetry,* New York: New Directions, 1935, pp. 4-5.

Hutchings, W., "Syntax of Death: Instability in Gray's 'Elegy Written in a Country Churchyard,'" in *Studies in Philology,* Vol. LXXXI, No. 4, Fall, 1984, pp. 496-514.

Johnson, Samuel, "Gray," in his *Lives of the English Poets,* Vol. II, 1781; reprinted by Oxford University Press, 1967, pp. 453-64.

Krutch, Joseph Wood, "Introduction," in *The Selected Letters of Thomas Gray* by Thomas Gray, edited by Joseph Wood Krutch, New York: Farrar, Strauss and Young, Inc., 1952, pp. ix-xxxii.

Weaver, Carl J., "The Bicentenary of Gray's 'Elegy,'" in *Colby Library Quarterly,* Series III, No. 1, February, 1951, pp. 9-12.

Weinfield, Henry, *The Poet Without a Name: Gray's "Elegy" and the Problem of History,* Carbondale: Southern Illinois University Press, 1991.

For Further Study

Brooks, Cleanth, "Gray's Storied Urn," in *The Well-Wrought Urn,* New York: Harcourt Brace, 1947, pp. 96-113.

> Brooks, one of this century's most esteemed literary critics, examines the layers of complexity in this seemingly simple poem, which he likens to "a tissue of allusion and half-allusion."

Glazier, Lyle, "Gray's *Elegy:* "The Skull Beneath the Skin," in *University of Kansas Review,* Vol. XIX, Spring, 1953, pp. 174-180.

> Glazier interprets this as a poem of equality, favoring no class over another. He reminds readers that it is not merely about the virtues of the poor, but a declaration that all persons, rich and poor, are mortal.

Golden, Morris, *Thomas Gray,* New York: Grosset … Dunlap, Publishers, 1964.

> This book-length overview of Gray's life and career provided students with a good general background of the poet's importance.

Hutchings, W., "Syntax of Death: Instability in Gray's *Elegy Written in a Country Churchyard,"* in *Thomas Gray's Elegy Written in a Country*

Churchyard, edited by Harold Bloom, Philadelphia: Chelsea House Publishers, 1987.

This essay gives a focused, scholarly look at Gray's use of language and punctuation, with ample references to other poems and other critics' thoughts.

McCarthy, B. Eugene, *Thomas Gray: The Progress of a Poet,* Madison, NJ: Fairleigh Dickinson University Press, 1997.

McCarthy examines the development of Gray's life and thought, giving special attention to his translations and, of course, the "Elegy."

Milton Keynes UK
Ingram Content Group UK Ltd.
UKHW021053200324
439767UK00015B/463

9 781375 379397